COSTA RICAN TYPICAL FOODS

Carmen de Musmanni
Lupita de Weiler

Questions or comments at:
crtypicalfoods@hotmail.com

Printed in Costa Rica, 2009
by Impresos Rápidos / Teléfono: 2552-6868
Reg. Pend.

CONTENTS

Side Dishes and Vegetables

4

Ceviche de Corvina

(Marinated White Seabass)

1 lb. Seabass, cut in small pieces
3 tablespoons onion, finely chopped
1 tablespoons celery finely chopped
2 tablespoons fresh coriander, chopped
2 cups lemon juice
Salt, pepper and Tabasco Sauce® to taste
1/2 teaspoons Worcester Sauce

Combine all ingredients in a glass bowl. Let stand for at least four hours in the refrigerator.

Serve chilled in small bowls topped with catsup and soda crackers on the side.
8 Servings.

Ceviche de Mango

(Marinated Mango)

8-10 very green mangoes, peeled and finely diced.
2 tablespoons catsup
1/2 teaspoon mustard
1/4 teaspoon freshly ground black pepper
2 tablespoons onion, finely chopped
1 teaspoon salt
2 teaspoons Worcester Sauce

Combine all ingredients, refrigerate. Serve with soda crackers as an hors d'oeuvre.

Guacamole
(Avocado Dip)

2 ripe avocados, peeled and finely chopped
1 small tomato, skinned and chopped
juice of 1 lemon
2 tablespoons onion, finely chopped
1/2 teaspoon salt
2 tablespoons fresh coriander, chopped
Tabasco to taste
1/2 teaspoon Worcester Sauce

Combine all ingredients in an electric blender. Process until mixture is lumpy.

Note: If not made just before serving, put the avocado pits in the mixture to prevent darkening.

Serve with hot tortillas or tortilla chips as an hors d'oeuvre.

Empanada de Queso
(Corn Cheese Patty)

2 cups corn mixture (Masa)
1/2 teaspoon salt
1/2 cup grated white cheese
Dash of Tabasco Sauce® optional

Mix the Masa with salt and Tabasco Sauce®. Form balls of 1 1/2 tablespoons of the corn mixture. Put between two plastic sheets and press with a small pan to form a thin pancake. Put 1 1/4 teaspoons grated cheese into the center and fold in half. Seal softly with finger tips and fry in oil until golden.

About 2 dozen.

Tortillas de Queso

(Cheese Tortillas)

2 cups corn mixture (Masa)
1/2 cup white cheese
1/4 teaspoon salt
Oil

Mix cheese with masa and form balls of 1 1/2 table-spoons. Put each ball it between 2 plastic sheets and press with a small pan to form a thin pancake, can also be made by hand or with a tortilla maker.

Toast over medium heat in a pan or comal (special pan), after cooking each tortilla, clean the pan with a paper towel dampened in oil.

About 2 Dozen.

Chorreadas
(Corn Pancakes)

2 cups fresh corn kernels
1/2 cup sugar
1/4 cup flour
2 eggs
2 tablespoons butter
1/2 cup milk
1/2 teaspoons vanilla, optional
Oil or butter

Combine all ingredients in a blender until mixture is lumpy. Fry in butter or oil forming pancakes. Serve hot and top with cream cheese or sour cream.

Yields between 12 to 20 depending or size.

Gallo de Carne
(Meat Appetizer)

1/2 kg cooked shredded beef, seasoned to taste
20 corn tortillas
1 recipe Cabbage Salad; page 13
Hot peppers

Warm tortillas until soft. Place 1 tablespoon of seasoned meat in the center and top with cabbage salad. Garnish with hot peppers, if desired.

Gallo de chorizo
(Sausage Appetizer)

Same as Gallo de Carne, but substitute a small piece of cooked, drained chorizo sausage for the shredded beef.

Gallo de Picadillo
(Hash Appetizer)

Warm tortillas and fill with 1 tablespoon of any of the picadillos on page 44.

Palmito Gratinado
(Heart of Palm au Gratin)

1 can palmito
1 cup half & half
1/2 cup parmesan cheese, grated
1 teaspoon bread crumbs

Preheat oven to 400 F
Rinse palmito thoroughly to take away the vinegar flavor. Cut into 1/2 inch rounds and place in a large shallow Pyrex dish (or four individual oven proof glass dishes). Cover with half & half and top with parmesan cheese and bread crumbs. Bake about 10 minutes at 400 F and serve inmediately.
4 Servings.

Ensalada de Repollo
(Cabbage Salad)

2 cups cabbage, shredded
1 cup diced ripe tomato
3 tablespoons fresh coriander, finely chopped
2 teaspoons lemon juice
2 teaspoons olive oil
1/2 teaspoon salt
Dash of freshly ground black pepper

Mix all ingredients together. Serve inmediately.

6 Servings.

Crema de maíz

(Cream of Corn)

1 can of corn
1 cup half & half
1 cup milk
1 envelope chicken broth or 2 bouillon cubes
1/2 tablespoon butter or margarine
1 tablespoon of flour
1 teaspoon flour
1/2 teaspoon salt
Dash of freshly ground black pepper
Grated parmesan cheese to garnish

Drain corn and mix half of it with all other ingredients. Blend for 1 minute. Place in bowl. Bring to a boil at medium heat, stirring constantly. Add the remaining corn. Garnish with parmesan cheese.
4 Servings.

Crema de Pejibaye

(Cream of Pejibaye)

6 cooked pejibayes, peeled and seeded
1 cup half & half
1 cup milk
1 envelope chicken broth or 2 cubes bouilon
1 teaspoon onion, minced
1/2 teaspoon butter or margarine
1 teaspoon flour
1 teaspoon fresh parsley, finely chopped
1/2 teaspoon salt
Dash of freshly ground black pepper

Place all ingredients in blender, except parsley. Blend for 1 minute. Strain into pot. Bring to a boil at medium heat, stirring constantly. Sprinkle with parsley.

4 Servings.

Sopa Negra

(Black Bean Soup)

2 cups black beans
6 cups water
2 tablespoon onion, finely chopped
2 cloves garlic, finely chopped
1 teaspoon salt
2 tablespoon fresh coriander, finely chopped
4 hard boiled eggs, minced
1 tablespoon Worcester Sauce

Cook black beans in salt water with coriander, onion and garlic for 45 minutes in pressure cooker. Strain, and set broth aside. Blend 1 cup of beans and return to brth. Add Worcester Sauce and the rest of the beans to a boil. Garnish with minced hard boiled eggs. Best if made the day before.

6 Servings.

Sopa de Tortilla

(Tortilla Soup)

5 cups homemade hot chicken soup
Dash of Tabasco Sauce
2 cups chopped tortillas
Oil
1/2 cup tomato, diced
1/2 cup avocado, diced
1/4 cup coriander, chopped
1/4 cup onion, chopped
1/4 cup diced hot peppers

Fry tortillas in oil. Drain on a paper towel. Place fried tortillas bits in soup dishes and laddle soup on top. Serve inmediately.

Serve the tomato, avocado, coriander, hot peppers and onion in separate dishes for people to top the soup with them as desired.

4 Servings.

Arroz con Chancho
(Pork Rice)

2 cups rice
1/2 kg pork sirloin
1/2 cup onion, chopped
3 tablespoon bell pepper, finely chopped
1 teaspoon garlic powder
5 tablespoons oil
1/2 teaspoon achiote
1 cup string beans, cooked and sliced
1 cup carrots, cooked and diced
1 teaspoon Worcester Sauce
1/2 teaspoon salt
Freshly ground pepper to taste
1/4 cup raisins, optional

Cut the pork in 1 inch cubes. Cook over medium heat with 2 cups water, salt, pepper, garlic powder and Worcester Sauce, until tender (about 45 minutes).

In a separate skillet, saute the onions, bell peppers and achiote in oil. Add this mixture, the rice and 3 cups hot water to the meat and cook until rice is done. Then add vegetables and raisins and mix with a fork.
8 Servings.

Arroz con Palmito

(Heart of Palm Rice)

3 cups white rice, cooked
1 large can palmito, drained and diced
2 cups bechamel sauce
2 cups tomato sauce
1 cup white cheese, grated
1/4 cup parmesan cheese, grated
1 teaspoon bread crumbs

Preheat oven to 375 F.
Combine palmito and bechamel sauce. In a large deep Pyrex, put a layer of 1/3 rice, then a layer of 1/3 bechamel sauce, then a layer of 1/3 tomato sauce and top with 1/3 cheese. Repeat layers three times. Garnish top with parmesan and bread crumbs. Bake at 375 F for 15 minutes or until golden brown. Serve immediately.
10 Servings.

Arroz con Pollo

(Chicken Rice)

1 chicken
3 cups rice
2 tablespoons onion, finely chopped
1 tablespoons bell pepper, finely chopped
1/2 cup cooked peas
1/2 cup cooked carrots, diced
1/2 cup cooked string beans, sliced
2 tablespoons raisins
2 tablespoons green olives, sliced
1/4 teaspoon achiote
2 teaspoons Worcester Sauce
2 tablespoons oil
Salt to taste
Coriander leaves to garnish

Cook chicken with 1/2 the onion and 1/2 the bell pepper, salt, and 4 cups water until tender. Let cool. Strain the juice and add water to make 5 cups. Discard bones and shred the chicken. In a large pot, heat oil with achiote and saute the remaining onion, and bell pepper. Add the rice, vegetables, chicken juice, chicken, and water mixture. Cook until rice is done, add raisins and olives. Fluff with a fork Garnish with coriander leaves.
8 Servings.

Bistec encebollado
(Onion Steak)

6 sirloin beef steaks
6 medium onions, peeled and sliced
1/2 teaspoon garlic powder
1 teaspoon Worcester Sauce
1/2 teaspoon salt
1/4 teaspoon freshly ground pepper
2 tablespoons oil
2 tablespoons butter or margarine

Prepare meat with garlic, Worcester Sauce, salt and pepper. Set aside. In a large skillet, brown onion in butter and oil until golden. Remove onion from skillet and set aside on a plate. Place steaks in skillet at high temperature. Fry on both sides to desired doneness. Place steaks on serving plate. Return onions to hot skillet with meat dripping for one minute, stirring well. Top meat with onions. Serve inmediately.
6 Servings.

Mondongo en Salsa
(Tripe)

1 1/2 kg. tripe, washed and cut into 1/2" strips
1/4 kg ham hock
2 tablespoons onion, finely chopped
2 tablespoons fresh coriander, finely chopped
2 cloves garlic, finely chopped
2 peeled potatoes, diced
2 peeled carrots, diced
2 medium tomatoes, blended
2 teaspoons salt
1/2 teaspoon freshly ground pepper
3 tablespoons Worcester Sauce
1 1/2 cups water

Put everything in a pressure cooker except the carrots and potatoes. Cook 1 hour•. Add carrots, cook for 15 minutes, add potatoes and cook until done. Optional: add a can of garbanzo beans (chick-peas).

• Sometimes it is necesary to add water at this point. Serve with white rice.
8-10 Servings.

Olla de Carne
(Boiled Beef and Vegetables)

3/4 kg lean stewing beef
1/4 kg beef ribs
5 cups water
1/2 cup onion, finely chopped
1/2 green pepper, finely chopped
1/2 cup coriander, finely chopped
1 chayote peeled and quartered
1 green plantain cut in 4 chunks
1 ripe plantain cut in 4 chunks
1/2 kg yuca peeled and cut into 4 pieces
1 sweet potato, peeled and quartered
3 potatoes peeled and quartered
2 tiquizques peeled and halved
1/4 kg ripe summer squash, in chunks
1/2 teaspoon fresh thyme
2 teaspoons salt
2 tablespoons Worcester Sauce
2 ears corn cut into 1 inch rounds
1/2 teaspoon Tabasco Sauce ®

Cut meat into pieces and simmer in water with green pepper, onion, coriander, Worcester Sauce, Tabasco Sauce®, and salt over low heat 1 1/2 hours. Never allow to boil. Strain broth and add the vegetables and meat. Simmer for 1 hour or until all vegetables are done. Best if made 1 day ahead of serving. Serve with white rice.

8 Servings.

Tortas de carne
(Meat and Corn Patties)

1/2 kg ground beef
1/4 kg ground pork
1/2 cup onions, minced
2 tablespoons bell pepper, minced
2 tablespoons fresh coriander, minced
2 cloves garlic, minced
1 tablespoon Worcester Sauce
3/4 cup corn mixture (Masa)
1 teaspoon freshly ground pepper
1 egg
Oil

Combine all ingredients except oil. Let rest of 2 hours for flavors to blend. Form small patties and fry in hot oil. Serve on hot tortillas and top with shredded cabbage, tomato, lemon juice and Tabasco Sauce®.

20 two inch patties.

Frijoles blancos con chancho

(White Beans wih Pork)

1/2 kg pork sirloin
1/2 kg pork spareribs
1 kg white beans
1 cup potatoes, diced
1 cup carrots, diced
2 tablespoons onion, finely chopped
2 tablespoons green pepper, finely chopped
2 tablespoons coriander, finely chopped
2 teaspoons salt
2 tablespoons Worcester Sauce
1/2 teaspoon freshly ground pepper

Cut pork into 1 inch cubes. Cut ribs into pieces. Wash beans
and put all together in a pan with green pepper, potatoes,
coriander, salt, Worcester Sauce and 4 cups water. Simmer
3 hours over low heat. Add potatoes and carrots and simmer
for an additional 1/2 hour.
10 Servings.

Chilaquilas

(Tortilla and Meat Patties)

2 cups cooked shredded meat, well seasoned
20 tortillas
5 eggs, beaten
3 cups tomato sauce
3 cups cheese grated
Oil

Preheat ovn to 350 F.
Fill each tortilla with meat and fold in half. Dip each folded tortilla in the beaten egg and fry. Arrange in an oven proof dish, cover with tomato sauce and cheese. Bake at 350 F for 15 minutes.
6 Servings.

Tacos Ticos
(Costa Rican Tacos)

1/2 Kg cooked beef, shredded
20 corn tortillas
Oil
2 cups shredded cabbage
1 cup tomato, cubed
1 teaspoon fresh coriander, finely chopped
1/2 cup cheese, grated
Tabasco Sauce® to taste

Fill each tortilla with meat, roll half way and hold with a toothpick. Fry in oil until golden. Drain in paper towels. Top with cabbage, tomato, cheese and sauce. Tabasco Sauce if desired. Serve immediately.
20 Servings.

Sauce

1/2 cup catsup
1/2 cup mayonnaise
1 teaspoon mustard
1 teaspoon lemon juice
1/2 tablespoon Worcester Sauce

Combine all ingredients and spoon over the hot tacos.

Chile Relleno
(Stuffed Bell Pepper)

4 bell peppers
1/4 kg ground beef
1/2 cup onion, chopped
1/2 teaspoon garlic powder
1/4 cup fresh coriander, chopped
2 eggs
1/2 tablespoon Worcester Sauce
Dash of Tabasco Sauce®
Salt and freshly ground pepper to taste
Oil

Coat bell pepper with oil and broil on all sides until skin curls. Remove from oven, let cool. Peel and remove seeds. Cook ground beef with oil, onion, garlic powder coriander, Worcester Sauce, Salt, pepper and Tabasco Sauce®. Fill bell peppers with meat mixture. Beat eggs, dip peppers in them and fry in oil on all sides.
Serve immediately.
4 Servings.

Papa Rellena
(Stuffed Potatoes)

6 large cooked potatoes
1 cup cooked ground beef, well seasoned
3 eggs beaten
2 cups tomato sauce
1/2 cup grated cheese

Preheat oven to 350 F.
Cut potatoes in half. Scoop the inside of the potato out and place in dish with the meat and cheese. Mix well. Fill hollowed potato shells with the mixture. Dip in egg and fry. Place in oven proof dish. Cover with tomato sauce and bake at 350 F for 15 minutes.
6 Servings.

Papas con chorizo
(Potatoes with Pork Sausage)

6 medium potatoes peeled and quartered
1/2 kg pork sausage
1/2 teaspoon achiote (paprika)
1/4 teaspoon salt
1/4 teaspoon Worcester Sauce

Skin pork sausage and cut into two inch pieces. Cook sausage slowly in casserole for 15 minutes. Pour off some of the grease from the pork sausage. Add achiote, potatoes, Worcester Sauce, 1 cup of hot water and salt and cook over low heat 45 minutes. Serve hot with rice.

6 Servings.

Gallo Pinto

(Rice and Beans)
The traditional Costa Rican Dish

3 cups «day old» cooked rice
2 cups freshly cooked black beans
2 tablespoons onion, finely chopped
1 tablespoon bell pepper, finely chopped
2 tablespoons fresh coriander, finely chopped
3 strips bacon, cooked, drained, crumbled
2 tablespoons oil
1/2 tablespoon Worcester Sauce
1/2 tablespoon Tabasco Sauce®, optional

Saute onion and bell pepper in oil in medium heat. Add
beans and cook 2 minutes longer. Add rice and mix,
cook 3 minutes more. Add Worcester Sauce. Tabasco
Sauce ® and coriander, mix well. Garnish with bacon
crumbs. If desired, top with sour cream.

6 Servings.

Rice and Beans

(Caribbean Version of Gallo Pinto)

1 lb rice
1/2 lb beans (red or black eye)
1 large coconut or 1 bag of shredded coconut

Blend the coconut meat (not the coconut milk) with two cups of warm water.

In large pot cook the beans with this mixture, one garlic clove and a dash of thyme. If necessary add water. Cook until tender (more or less one hour). When beans are done add rice, mix and cook until rice is done.

Better if rice is cooked in the oven.
Note: Tradionally red beans are used to serve with chicken and black-eye beans with fish.

TAMALES

The traditional Christmas tamal is on the table of every Costa Rican. The making ot them is almost a ceremony that encompasses the entire family.

All tamales in Costa rica are wrapped in banana or plantain leaves for cooking. This contributes a lot to the flavor. In the USA yo may substitute aluminum foil for the banana leaves, in which case we advise you to put a grape leaf in each tamal to add to the flavor.

Masa de Tamal
(Same for every tamal)

2 1/2 kg Masa (corn dough)
1 cup concentrated pork broth
1 cup concentrated chicken broth
4 chicken bouillon cubes
1 tablespoon Worcester Sauce
6 strips bacon, cooked and crumbled, including fat
1/2 teaspoon pepper
2 cups potatoes, mashed

Combine all ingredients, mix well. Bring to boil on low heat, stirring constantly to prevent sticking. Remove from heat as soon as it starts to boil.

Tamal Navideño
(Christmas Tamal)

Take 2 pieces of banana leaf, 1 square foot each, place
3 tablespoons of dough in the center. Place on top of
dough:

1 small piece cooked pork
1 small piece cooked chicken
4-5 green peas
1 green olive
4-5 raisings
1 small piece cooked carrot
4-5 capers
1 strip bell pepper
4-5 garbanzo beans (chick - peas)
1 teaspoon cooked achiote* rice

Wrap up the sides of the leaves, forming a brick shape.
Place 2 tamales together, seams facing inward, and tie
with string or twine. Place the tied tamales in hot water
and boil for 1/2 hour. Serve hot. Store in refrigerator.
25 Servings.

* Achiote is paprika powder.

Tamal de frijoles
(Black Bean Tamal)

On two small (8"x8") banana leaves, layered, place 1
tablespoon Masa dough. Add 2 teaspoons of «frijoles
molidos», see recipe page 48, and hot peppers to taste.
Wrap and cook as in recipe above.

Tamal de Verduras
(Vegetable Tamal)

Replace «frijoles molidos» with cooked mustard greens
and potatoes.

Empanadas de Plátano

(Plantain and Cheese Patties)

4 ripe plantains
2 teaspoons sugar
Butter or margarine
1/2 cup precessed American cheese, grated
1/2 cup frijoles molidos, optional
Oil

Peel, boil and mash plantains. Add sugar and mix well. Shape the plantain mixture into 8 flat thin patties. Spread cheese and beans over the patties. Fold patties in half and press edges together. Fry in oil and butter until golden brown on both sides. Serve hot.
8 Patties.

Plátanos Empanizados
(Breaded Plantains)

1 egg, beaten
1 teaspoon salt
1/2 cup evaporated milk
3 ripe plantains
1 cup cornflake crumbs or cracker crumbs
Oil

In a heavy skillet put oil 1 1/2 to 2 inches. Combine salt, egg and milk. Peel plantains and cut into 1 inch rounds. Dip plantain slices in milk mixture, then roll in crumbs until well covered. Fry in oil, preheated to 375 F, until brown and fork tender. Drain on paper towels and serve hot as a vegetable.
6 Servings.

Plátano Frito

(Fried Plantains)

3 large, very ripe plantains
Oil
Margarine

Be sure plantains are very ripe, preferably turning black. If not, hit all over with a wooden spoon to soften.

Peel and slice the plantains in 1/2 inch rounds. Fry in half oil half margarine at medium heat until golden. Serve hot. To keep warm, sprinkle with sugar and place in warm oven.

6 Servings.

Plátanos en Gloria
(Glorious Plantains)

3 ripe plantains
2-4 tablespoons butter or margarine
1 teaspoon oil
1/2 teaspoon salt
1/4 lb mild cheese, grated
1/2 - 1 cup cream
1/4 cup parmesan cheese, grated

Preheat oven to 350 F

Peel plantains and slice diagonally 1/4 inch thick. Fry slices lightly in butter until brown on both sides. Drain on paper towels and sprinkle with salt. In buttered casserole, arrange alternate layers of plantains and grated mild cheese, finishing with a cheese layer. Pour cream over top until it shows through the top layer of cheese. Sprinkle with parmesan cheese. Bake in moderate 350 F, oven until firm but not dry, about 45 minutes.
4-6 Servings.

Plátanos en Miel

(Candied Plantains)

3 large ripe plantains
1 cup sugar
1 1/2 cup water
1 tablespoon oil
1 tablespoon butter or margarine
1/2 teaspoon vanilla
Dash of cinnamon, optional

Hit the plantains on all sides with a wooden spoon to soften. Peel and cut into 5 pieces each. In a large skillet, melt butter and oil on high heat, add plantains, Fry until brown. Combine sugar, vanilla, cinnamon, and water. Reduce heat to low, and pour liquid over the plantains. Continue cooking until the liquid thickens, about 15 minutes.

4-5 Servings.

Chancletas
(«Old shoes» - Stuffed Mexican Squash)

3 large, very ripe chayotes
1/2 cup shredded white cheese
1 tablespoon butter or margarine
2 tablespoons bread crumbs
1/4 cup parmesan cheese, grated
1 tablespoon half & half
1 teaspoon salt
Cream Cheese

Optional: 1/2 tablespoon raisins
            12 teaspoon vanilla
             1 teaspoon sugar

Cook chayotes whole in the pressure cooker in 2 cups water and salt for 20 minutes. Drain, let cool.
Cut chayotes in half, discard seeds. Carefully scoop out the pulp, place it in a bowl and mash it, add cheese, butter and cream. Mix well. Spoon pulp cheese mixture into the hollow chayote shells. Sprinkle with bread crumbs and parmesan cheese, bake at 375 F until golden. Top each with a dollop of cream cheese.
6 Servings.

Enyucado

(Mandioc Patty)

1/2 Kg yuca
2 chicken bouillon cubes
1 cup cooked ground beef, well seasoned
1/2 up white cheese, grated
Oil

Peel, wash and cook yuca in hot water with the chicken bouillon. When very tender, drain and smash into a puree. Form balls, press finger into the ball to form a hole in the middle. Stuff with meat and cheese, then close the hole with yuca. Shape ball into a roll being careful that the meat remains covered with yuca. Fry in oil on all sides unitl golden. Serve inmediately.

About 12 Servings.

Yuca Frita

(Fried Mandioc)

1/2 kg yuca
2 chicken bouillon cubes
2 tablespoons butter or margarine
1 tablespoon oil

Peel and wash yuca thoroughly. Cut in 3 inch rounds.
Heat water and bouillon in a large pot. Gently place
yuca in boiling water and cook until tender. Drain and
place pieces on end and cut into 6 sections each. Fry on
all sides in melted oil and butter until golden brown.
Serve immediately.
4 Servings.

Also used as a «boca»

Patacones

(Green Plantain Crisps)

4 green plantains
1 teaspoon salt
Oil

Peel plantains and cut into 6 rounds each. Fry in hot oil until golden. Place on cutting board and smash the plantains with a glass bottle or rolling pin. Sprinkle with salt and return to pan to fry again. Fry until crispy. Drain on paper towels and serve immediately.

Traditionally served with white cheese and Frijoles Molidos (Black Bean Dip, page 48)
6-8 Servings.

Picadillo de Plátano
(Green Plantain Hash)

4 green plantains
1/4 kg ground beef
2 tablespoons onion, finely chopped
2 tablespoons fresh coriander, finely chopped
2 cloves garlic, finely chopped
1/2 cup tomato, minced
1 teaspoons Worcester Sauce
1 1/2 teaspoon salt
1/2 teaspoon freshly ground pepper
Dash oil of Tabasco Sauce ®
Oil

Peel plantains and cut in three pieces each. Cook in water with 1 teaspoon of salt until tender. Let cool and mince. Set aside in a large skillet, cook the meat with onion, garlic, 1/2 teaspoon salt, and pepper, use oil as needed. When done, add remaining ingredients and cook 10 minutes.
Serve as a vegetable or on hot tortillas as a «boca».
8 Servings

Picadillo de Papa
(Potato Hash)

1/2 kg potatoes, peeled and diced
1/4 kg pork sausage, peeled
2 tablespoons fresh coriander, finely chopped
1/2 teaspoon Worcester Sauce
Dash of Tabasco Sauce®
1/4 cup water

Saute sausage 10 minutes over medium heat, then crumble. Drain on paper towels. Return to pan, add remaining ingredients, stir, cover and cook until potatoes are done. Serve with hot tortillas.
8 Servings.

Picadillo de chayote
(Mexican Squash Hash)

3 chayotes, peeled and diced
1/4 kg ground beef
2 tablespoons onion, finely chopped
2 tablespoons fresh coriander, finely chopped
2 cloves garlic, finely chooped
1 teaspoon freshly ground pepper
1 teaspoon oil

Saute the meat in oil with onion, garlic, salt and pepper until lightly brown. Add remaining ingredients, cover and cook until chayote is tender. Serve as a vegetable or on hot tortillas.

8 Servings.

Zapallitos Rellenos
(Stuffed Green Squash)

4 zapallitos (green squash)
1 hard boiled egg, finely chopped
1/4 cup cheese, grated
1/4 cup half & half
1/4 cup parmesan cheese, grated
1/2 teaspoon salt
1/4 cup bread crumbs

Boil the zapallitos in salt water until tender. Let cool. Cut in half lengthwise. Scoop the inside meat into a strainer. With a spoon, force the liquid throuh until only and squash paste remains. Combine squash paste, egg, grated cheese, half & half and mix well. Fill zapallito shells with paste mixture and sprinkle with parmesan cheese and bread crumbs. Bake at 350 F for 8 minutes, then broil until brown. Serve inmediately.

4 Servings.

Guiso de Maíz (Ajiaco)
(Corn Stew)

2 cups fresh cut corn
1 cup chayote, diced
1/2 cup milk
1 chicken bouillon cube
2 tablespoons fresh coriander, chopped
1 teaspoon sugar
1 tablespoon butter or margarine
Dash of freshly ground pepper

Combine all ingredients and cook over medium heat until vegetables are done. Serve as a vegetable.
6 Servings.

Huevos con tortilla

(Tortilla Eggs)

1 package tortillas (12)
4 eggs, beaten
1/2 teaspoon salt
Dash of pepper
Butter or margarine

Cut tortillas into small pieces, approximately 1 inch squares, fry them in butter over medium heat until crispy. Add eggs, salt and pepper and cook to desired doneness.

4 Servings.

Frijoles molidos

(Black Bean Dip)

4 cups cooked black beans
1/2 cup onion, finely chopped
1/4 cup coriander, finely chopped
2 cloves garlic, finely chopped
4 strips bacon, cooked and crumbled
1/4 cup sour cream
1 teaspoon Tabasco Sauce®
1 tablespoon sugar
1 tablespoon Worcester Sauce

Blend beans in electric blender until consistency is creamy. Saute onion and garlic in bacon fat until brown. Add all ingredients except bacon and sour cream. Cook over medium heat until boiling, stir occasionally to prevent sticking. Remove from heat at least 10 minutes before serving to allow thickening. Top with sour cream and bacon. Serve with hot tortillas or corn chips. This dish is traditionally served with Arroz con Pollo or as an hors d'oeuvre,
8 Servings.

FRESCOS

The typical Costa Rican family has a different fresco with lunch each day. Our country is blessed with an immense variety of tropical fruits which are the base of all frescos. These are a great source of vitamins and a great treat for everyone.

These delicious, nutritious drinks are easily made by placing the fruit, water and suggar to taste, in the blender. Blend for a few minutes, add chopped ice and serve.

Frescos made with the following fruits must be strained; pineapple, cas, maracuya, guisaro, naranjilla, carambola, blackberry (mora), guanabana (sour sap), guayaba, marañon.

The following frescos do not need to be strained; fresa (strawberry), papaya, cantaloupe, mango, watermelon.

Papaya, blackberry, banana and guanabana can be made with milk instead of water for a rich change of taste.

Tamarindo should be first boiled. Then left to rest for 1 hour and strained.

Chan should be washed, placed in water, left to rest for 1 hour and it is then ready to drink.

Fresco made with tangerine, grapefruit or orange is made the same as lemonade, with sugar to taste.

Fresco de Frutas
(Mixed fruit refreshment)

2 cups mixed fruit, chopped (orange, banana, papaya, pineapple).

Mix fruit in a large pitcher of water and add 1/2 cup «sirope» (a strawberry flavored liquid candy) and ice.

Ponche
(Hot Punch)

4 cups milk
2 egg yolks
sugar to taste
1/2 teaspoon vanilla
2 teaspoons corn starch
Ground cinnamon, optional
°Rum or Brandy, optional

Combine all ingredients, except liquor in a saucepan. Bring to a boil over low heat stirring constantly. Add liquor and beat with a whisk or an electric beater until foamy. Sprinkle with cinnamon. Serve very hot. 4 Servings.

Note: In the old days, people had dinner between 5:00 and 6:00 in the evening. Before going to bed, around 8:30, they always had a cup of hot «ponche». Today it is still given to children, old folks, and convalescent people. It is said to help you sleep well.

Flan de Coco

(Coconut Flan)

1 can condensed milk
1 can evaporated milk
1/2 cup sugar
1/2 cup milk
1/2 cup fresh coconut, shredded
6 eggs

Combine all ingredients in an electric blender for 3 minutes. Pour mixture in caramelized Pyrex dish and bake in a double boiler at 350 F for 45 minutes or until knife comes out clean. Let cool, run knife around the edge of the dish to separate it from the sides.
Refrigerate.
12 Servings.

Miel de coco

(Coconut Sweet)

1 fresh coconut, hulled and shredded
1 cup coconut milk
1 cup sugar
1 cup milk
1 tablespoon butter or margarine
1/2 teaspoon vanilla

Combine all ingredients and cook over medium heat, stirring constantly until the bottom of the pan shows when stirred. Let cool.
Delicious over vanilla ice cream.
8 Servings.

Rosquillas de Maizena®
(Cornstarch Cookies)

2 cups flour
2 tablespoons cornstarch
1 egg
1 cup butter or margarine
1 cup sugar

Preheat oven to 325 F.
Combine all ingredients, mix to form a smooth dough.
Roll into long strips 1/4 inch thick. Cut with a knife into
2 inch lengths, and form a ring with each piece. Place
the rings on an ungreased cookie sheet and sprinkle
with sugar. Bake at 325 F for 8 to 10 minutes. If
desired, sprinkle with cinnamon.
About 3 Dozen.

Tamal de Elote

(Corn Pudding)

1 can condensed milk
2 can whole kernel corn
3 eggs
1 cup melted butter or margarine
1 teaspoon cinnamon

Preheat oven to 350 F.
Combine all ingredients in an electric blender and blend for three minutes. Pour into a greased Pyrex dish and bake at 350 F for 45 minutes or until knife comes out clean. Serve chilled.
12-16 Servings.

Arroz con leche
(Rice Custard)

2 cups rice
1 can condensed sweetened milk
1 can evaporated milk
2 cinnamon sticks
2 whole cloves
Dash of salt
3 cups water

Cook rice in salted water until tender. Add remaining ingredients and mix with a fork, simmer for 15 minutes. Serve warm.

Variations:

Add:
1/2 cup canned pineapple or
1/2 cup shredded coconut or
1/2 cup raisins.
Top with marmalade
Sprinkle with cinnamon

8 Servings.

Cajeta de Coco
(Coconut Fudge)

2 cups condensed milk
1 cup fresh coconut meat, shredded
1 cup butter or margarine
1/2 cup María cracker crumbs (graham cracker)
1/2 teaspoon vanilla

Combine all ingredients in a pan and cook on low heat, stirring constantly with a wooden spoon. Continue cooking 5-6 minutes after boil has been reached. Form small balls and place on paper cups.
20-30 Fudge Balls.

Cajeta de Leche
(Milk Fudge)

1 can condensed milk
1 cup powdered milk
1 1/2 tablespoons butter or margarine

Combine all ingredients and stir with a wooden spoon until smooth. Form small balls and place them in small paper cups*. With a knife cut a cross on the top of each ball. In the center of the cross place one of the following:

whole clove
piece of macadamia nut
slice of almond
piece of candied fruit

15-20 Fudge Balls.

*Traditionally the balls were placed on lemon leaves to absorb the lemon flavor.

Tres Leches

(Milk Cake)

Cake Base
5 eggs
1 teaspoon baking powder
1 cup sugar
1/2 teaspoon vanilla
1 1/2 cups flour

Beat the egg whites, until fluffy and set aside.

Beat the egg yolks with the sugar until creamy. Add vanilla, baking powder and flour (two tablespoons at a time), until well blended.

Fold the yolk mixture into the egg whites. Mix until well folded.

Pour into a greased rectangular Pyrex dish and bake for 30 minutes in a 350 F-preheated oven. Check that when you introduce a knife into the cake it comes out clean.

Let in cool and pierce all over with a fork.

Filling
2 cups milk
1 can condensed milk
1 can evaporated milk

Blend all three milks together and pour over the cool cake base.

Choose one of the following toppings for you cake:

Topping 1
1 1/2 cups half & half
1 teaspoon vanilla
1 cup sugar

Whip together until thick. Spread over top of the cake. Keep refrigerated.

Topping 2
4 egg whites
1 cup sugar
1/2 teaspoon vanilla
1/4 cup water

In a small saucepan put the sugar, vanilla and water. Cook over medium heat until you obtain a thick syrup (softball stage).

Beat egg whites until fluffy. While beating, pour the sugar mixture in a small but constant stream. Beat until you obtain a thick meringue style frosting.

Spread over top of the cake. Keep refrigerated.

12 servings

GLOSARY

Achiote: a natural red food coloring, an excellent source of vitamins. Similar to paprika.

Arroz: rice.

Boca: all types of appetizers, including canapes, hors d'oeuvres etc.

Cajeta: fudge.

Carambola: a star shaped tropical fruit used in making frescos.

Cas: a tropical fruit used in making frescos.

Ceviche: marinated raw fish, served as an appetizer.

Chan: seeds used in making frescos.

Chancho: pork.

Chayote: a Mexican squash, green or yellow.

Chile dulce: Bell pepper.

Chile picante: a small hot pepper.

Chilero: a tabasco like mixture, very hot.

Chilaquilas: tortilla and meat patties.

Chorizo: pork sausage.

Chorreadas: corn pancakes.

Coco: coconut.

Corvina: white seabass.

Elote:	corn on the cob.
Empanada:	latin pie, turnover.
Empanizado:	breaded.
Enyucado:	mandioc patty.
Fresa:	strawberry.
Fresco:	natural fruit drink
Gallo:	tortilla with filling.
Gallo Pinto:	rice and beans, the Costa Rican national dish.
Guacamole:	avocado dip.
Guanabana:	sour sap.
Güisaro:	a tropical fruit.
Guiso:	stew.
Maizena ®:	cornstarch.
Maíz:	corn.
Mango:	tropical fruit.
Maracuya:	tropical fuit used in frescos.
Marañon:	Fruit of the cashew nut.
Masa:	corn dough.
Melon:	cantaloupe.
Mondongo:	tripe.

Naranjilla: tropical fruit, a mixture between tomato and orange.

Palmito: heart of palm.

Papa: Potato.

Papaya: tropical fruit.

Patacones: green plantains, fried crisp.

Pejibaye: fruit of a palm.

Picadillo: hash.

Plátano: plantain, cooking banana.

Ponche: hot milk drink.

Rosquillas: ring shaped cookies.

Sandía: watermelon.

Tamarindo: a tropical fruit used in frescos. Comes in a brown brick shape, wrapped in plastic.

Ticos: diminutive name for Costa Ricans.

Torta: a patty.

Yuca: mandioc or cassava.

Zapallitos: baby squash

Notes:

_____

_____

_____

_____

_____

_____

_____

_____

_____

_____

_____

_____

_____

_____

_____

_____

_____

_____

_____

_____

641.59
M987c   Musmanni, Carmen de
Costa Rican typical foods/Carmen de Musmanni, Lupita
de Weiler, --1.ed.--San José: Productos Turísticos
Calu, 1994.
64 p.: il.;21cm.

ISBN 9968-9756-0-5
Impreso en: Impresos Rápidos, Cartago Costa Rica
1. Cocina. 2. Cocina costarricense. I. Weiler, Lupita de
II. Título.